ROBERT WILLIAMS

EX-GAY
CHRISTIAN

*Men and Women are Crowned
with God's Glory and Honor*

EX-GAY CHRISTIAN:
Men and Women are Crowned with God's Glory and Honor
Copyright © 2024 **Robert Williams**

ISBN (Paperback): 978-1-958475-85-0
ISBN (Ebook): 978-1-958475-86-7

PROMINENT
BOOKS

5830 E 2nd St, Ste 7000 #9983
Casper, WY 82609
USA

You have made him a little lower than the heavenly beings and crowned him with glory and honor. You have given him dominion over the works or your hands. You have put all things under his feet, all sheep and oxen, and the beasts of the field the birds of the heavens and the fish of the sea whatever passes along the paths of the seas.

—Psalm 8:5–8

CONTENTS

THE KINGDOM OF THIS WORLD SHALL BECOME THE LORD'S

SATAN IS PRESENTLY ruling the kingdom of this earth, the kingdom that he defrauded from Adam and Eve. Now, Satan dictates the unethical activities of this world by blinding the minds of those who have not accepted Christ's redemptive grace. His ploy blinds their minds and keeps them from realizing God's great plan to rescue His beloved creation through the sacrificial gift of His Son Jesus. Satan is aware should they gain knowledge of God's offer; he will not be able to keep them under his control. He aims to keep them in sin, so they'll accompany him to the judgment throne of Almighty God. He doesn't want to suffer eternal damnation by himself.

Jesus, our Great High Priest, and Savior is presently in heaven before the celestial Ark of the Covenant, which contains the ten commandments, ministers, and intercession for humanity's sins. He atones for every repentant soul desiring salvation and forgiveness for their transgressions, and those who will futuristically accept Christ's sacrifice or deny Him and gain eternal death for rejecting God's only remedy for the wayward sons and daughters of Adam and Eve.

Jesus presently makes attornment for the righteous dead and living and blots out their sins. He is the mediator between a sinful man and an offended God. What is Jesus doing? He stands between Almighty God and guilty man, protecting humanity from the righteous wrath of Almighty God. Nevertheless, one day, His call for salvation shall cease. There is a date scheduled on heaven's calendar when that appointment time is reached. At that time the angel will declare, "That there should be time no longer" (Rev. 10:6). That's when "the kingdom of the world has become the kingdom of our Lord and of his Messiah, and he will reign forever and ever" (Rev. 11:15). No one else gets saved at this period in history; it's over. Satan will have control of those rejecting Jesus's sacrifice. Then God's wrath, the plagues will be poured out upon the earth. Jesus, as the Great High Priest, has been holding back God's fury, which would have befallen sinful humanity. There will come a day when His intercession ceases. One day, our LORD will raise His hands and say, "He that is unjust, let him be unjust still: and he which is filthy, let him be filthy still: and he that is righteous, let him be righteous still: and he that is holy, let him be holy still (Rev. 22:11).

Then there will be nothing to hold back God's wrath. Then there will be a famine in the land:

> Not a famine of food or a thirst for water, but a famine of hearing the words of the LORD. People will stagger from sea to sea and wander from north to east, searching for the word of the LORD, but they will not find it. On that day the lovely young women and strong young men will faint because of thirst. (Amos 8:11–13)

This will be the time Satan will have control over the earth and those who were finally found to be unrepentant, rebellious on the earth, and there will be nothing to hold back the wrath of Almighty God.

Thank God, Jesus, our Great High Priest, is presently in heaven before the celestial Ark of the Covenant, which contains the Ten Commandments, ministering and making intercession for the sins of lost humanity. He atones for every soul desiring salvation and forgiveness for their transgressions; those who will futuristically accept Christ's sacrifice or those who will deny Him and gain eternal death for rejecting God's only remedy for the wayward sons and daughters of Adam.

Jesus presently makes attornment for the righteous dead and living and blots out their sins. He is the mediator between a sinful man and an offended God. What is Jesus doing? He stands between Almighty God and guilty man protecting humanity from the righteous wrath of God. Nevertheless, one day, His call for salvation shall cease. There is a date scheduled on earth's calendar, when we reach that appointed date, the angel will declare, "That there should be time no longer" (Rev. 10:6). That's when "the kingdom of the world has become the kingdom of our Lord and of his Messiah, and he will reign forever and ever" (Rev. 11:15). No one else gets saved; it's over.

Satan will have control of those rejecting His sacrifice. Then God's wrath, the plagues will be poured out upon the earth. Jesus was holding back God's fury. There will come a day when this intercession ceases. One day, our LORD will raise His hands and say, "He that is unjust, let him be unjust still: and he which is filthy, let him be filthy still: and he that is righteous, let him be righteous still: and he that is holy, let him be holy still" (Rev. 22:11).

There will be nothing to hold back God's wrath. Then there will be a famine throughout the land,

> Not a famine of food or a thirst for water, but a famine of hearing the words of the LORD. People will stagger from sea to sea and wander from north to east, searching for the word of the LORD, but they will not find it. In that day "the lovely young women and strong young men will faint because of thirst. (Amos 8:11–13)

This will be the time Satan will have control over the earth and those who were finally found to be unrepentant, rebellious on the earth; and there will be nothing to hold back the wrath of Almighty God.

CHRIST RETURNS AT THE LAST TRUMP

MOST CHRISTIANS FAIL to understand that the Rapture occurs at the very end of the tribulation when the seventh and last trumpet sounds. The Seventh Seal (Rev. 8:1) corresponds to the Harvest of the Great Multitude (Rev. 7:9–17). The Great multitudes are those who have come out of the extreme tribulation. In other words, they went through considerable tribulation, and the Harvest is post-tribulation. Their robes have been washed white in the blood of the Lamb—meaning, that they were Christians: "And they overcame him by the blood of the Lamb, and by the word of their testimony; and they loved not their lives unto the death" (Rev. 12:11). The Seventh Seal, the Seventh Trumpet, and the Seventh Bowl (Armageddon) correspond with the end of this age and the beginning of the Millennium (Rev. 11:15).

The rapture is said to take place in the twinkling of an eye (1 Cor. 15:51–2) at the Last Trumpet. When the Bowls of God's wrath are poured out, the Church is no longer on Earth. The Church is harvested by two angels in Revelations 14. Those who are harvested by the first angel appear in Heaven (Rev. 15). After this, the Bowls of God's wrath are poured out on those who remain on Earth after the rapture (Rev. 15–18).

THE COMING OF THE SON OF MAN

I SAW IN the night visions, and behold; one like the Son of man came with the clouds of heaven and came to the Ancient of days, and they brought him near before him.

And there was given him dominion, and glory, and a kingdom, that all people, nations, and languages, should serve him; His dominion is an everlasting dominion, which shall not pass away, and His kingdom that which shall not be destroyed. (Dan. 7:13-14)

24 But in those days, after that tribulation, the sun will be darkened, and the moon will not give its light;

25 the stars of heaven will fall, and the powers in the heavens will be shaken.

26 Then they will see the Son of Man coming in the clouds with great power and glory.

27 And then He will send His angels, and gather His elect from the four winds, from the farthest part of the earth to the farthest part of heaven. (Mark 13:24–27)

64 Jesus saith unto him, thou hast said: nevertheless, I say unto you, Hereafter shall ye see the Son of man sitting on the right hand of power, and coming in the clouds of heaven. (Matt. 26:64)

26 And then shall they see the Son of man coming in the clouds with great power and glory.

27 And then shall he send his angels and shall gather together his elect from the four winds, from the uttermost part of the earth to the uttermost part of heaven. (Mark 13:26–27)

JESUS RETURNS AT THE VERY END

14 For if we believe that Jesus died and rose again, even so, them also which sleep in Jesus will God bring with him.

15 For this we say unto you by the word of the Lord, that we which are alive and remain unto the coming of the Lord shall not prevent them which are asleep.

16 For the Lord himself shall descend from heaven with a shout, with the voice of the archangel, and with the trump of God: and the dead in Christ shall rise first:

17 Then we which are alive and remain shall be caught up together with them in the clouds, to meet the Lord in the air: and so shall we ever be with the Lord. (1 Thess. 4:14–17)

25 And there shall be signs in the sun, and in the moon, and in the stars; and upon the earth distress of nations, with perplexity; the sea and the waves roaring;

26 Men's hearts failing them for fear, and for looking after those things which are coming on the earth: for the powers of heaven shall be shaken.

27 And then shall they see the Son of man coming in a cloud with power and great glory. (Luke 21:25–27)

Comment: Christ returns at the very end. When we see signs in the sun, moon, and stars; distress of nations, the sea and waves roaring; the powers of heaven shaken; then the Son of man returns. Therefore, Jesus can't return until these events occur. He returns at the sound of the last trump.

EVENTS ASSOCIATED WITH THE BIBLICAL RETURN OF JESUS

THE HUMAN HEART REFLECTS HEAVEN

"ON EARTH AS in Heaven" (Matt. 6:10).

The common prophetic numbers are 4, 6, 7, 10, 12, and 70. The number 4 very often prophetically symbolizes foursquare or the world's wideness. The idea of universality is conveyed in the expressions "four corners of the earth" and "four winds of heaven" (Isa. 11:12; Jer. 49:36; Dan. 8:8; Rev. 7:1–2). For example, God's upright universal organization is symbolized by the four living creatures as described by both Ezekiel and John (Ezek. 1:5; Rev. 4:6).

The heart of Man is where the Almighty desires to place His throne. The heart, too, is composed of four chambers. To cite a few more examples: God's first four commandments deal explicitly with Him; four priests carry the Ark of the Covenant the Ark has four rings on it, and the center of the Ark is the mercy seat.

"And before the throne, there was a sea of glass like unto crystal: and in the midst of the throne, and round about the throne, were four beasts full of eyes before and behind" (Rev. 4:6).

The four beasts in Ezekiel 1 are described the same: Ezekiel has the same vision. He sees these four beasts bearing up the Ark of the Covenant. Again, there are four Levite priests required to carry Ark. All of this is an earthly representation of a heavenly scene.

CHRIST IN YOU, THE HOPE OF GLORY

"To them, God has chosen to make known among the Gentiles the glorious riches of this mystery, which is **Christ in you, the hope of glory**" (Col. 1:27).

Where in our clay temples does God reside? He lives within our hearts. His seat or throne is literally within the hearts of His children. There are four chambers in the human heart.

God told Moses exactly how to construct the Ark of the Covenant because it was to foreshadow His heavenly place of dwelling, a graphic representation of what John saw in heaven. He said I saw the four beasts and the Ark of the Covenant (the throne of God), and he saw twenty-four elders surrounding the throne (Rev. 4:6–9). Now, remember, God made us in that fashion: We have twenty-four ribs that surround the throne of God in our bodies. We really are the temple of the living God, "For I am fearfully, and wonderfully made" (Ps. 139:14).

Think of what God has done.

THIS IS A PICTURE OF THE ARK OF THE COVENANT

THE ARK OF the Covenant is known as the throne of God. "And there I will meet with you, and I will speak with you from above the mercy seat, from between the two cherubim which are on the ark of the Testimony, about everything which I will give you in commandment to the children of Israel" (Exod. 25:22).

So the outstretched wings of the cherubim were to provide a throne for God where He would mediate His rule on the earth as a representation of the real throne in heaven.

"So the people sent men to Shiloh, and they brought back the Ark of the Covenant of the LORD Almighty, who is enthroned between the cherubim" (1 Sam. 4:4 NIV).

When God had spoken to Moses out of the midst of the cloud upon Sinai, He also told him that He would come down to speak with him amid His people. It was from the area above the mercy seat that He did.

> Now when Moses went into the tabernacle of meeting
> to speak with Him, he heard the voice of One speaking to

him from above the mercy seat that was on the ark of the
Testimony, from between the two cherubim; thus, He spoke
to him. (Num. 7:89)

Jesus answered and said to them, "Destroy this temple,
and in three days I will raise it up."
Then the Jews said, "It has taken forty-six years to
build this temple, and will you raise it up in three days?"
(John 2:19–21)

But He was speaking of the temple of His body. They were looking
at the physical structure (Hebrew, *Mikdash*) of the temple, but when He
said, "Destroy this temple," He used the word in Hebrew *Mishkan*, which
was the word used in the Old Testament of the Presence that lit the holy
of holies on Yom Kippur in the tabernacle or temple. Jesus said I am the
temple (Mishkan) of God. When the glory (Hebrew, *Shechinah*) would
come down like a tornado or funnel, right through the roof of the holy of
holies, and the Presence would be manifested on the mercy seat between
the cherubim after the blood was sprinkled, that was the Mishkan. That
Presence was what Jesus said dwelt within Him. But the Ark above was
a type of shadow where God was planning to make His future dwelling
(within the very heart of His children). "For ye are the temple of the living
God; as God hath said, I will dwell in them, and walk-in them, and I will
be their God, and they shall be my people" (2 Cor. 6:16).

I have personally had a blessed experience in the past, and I was totally
oblivious to just what God was doing. It was during a tent revival, which
was being held in the Bronx, NY, in the summer of 1971. It happened
during the service when Rev. Don Stewart asked the congregation to give
an offering. Minister Stewart said, "God said to bring your very best gift,
and come across the platform praising God." Well, in the past, I received
many spiritual blessings when I obeyed God during the offering service.
This occasion was no different. I just believed what the prophet was saying,

and I crossed the platform, praising the Lord for His goodness. I gave my best and continued to my seat.

When I reached my seat, the minister said, "God said that the last group of people should come back across the platform, again praising the Lord, and He's going to bless you."

Well, all five of us obeyed the prophet, and God, and did just as He said. The power of the Holy Spirit was very intense. It was so powerful that we could barely make it down the steps from the platform. We held on to the railing because the power was tremendous. It was as if a huge magnet was pulling us toward this warm presence at the bottom of the platform. All five of us struggled to keep from falling over there. With our arms raised toward heaven, we felt the power emanating from God's presence. It was like a huge orb hovering above the platform with tremendous power beaming from it. I opened my eyes to get a glimpse, but I saw nothing.

Suddenly, I felt the presence of a cloud entering my chest. The only way I can describe it is that it was like a small, powerful tornado or funnel spinning in my chest, so much so that it almost tickled a bit. I had no idea what God was doing, but I understand now it was the *Shechinah* presence of the Holy Spirit taking possession of my human temple.

And in fact, Paul said about the church, "Know ye not that you are the temple (Mishkan) of God?" We, as the body of Christ, have the same Presence dwelling within us. God doesn't dwell in buildings now but within His people.

Romans 10:9 says, "That if you confess with your mouth the Lord Jesus and believe in your heart that God has raised Him from the dead, you will be saved." It's that easy. At that point, you become the Mishkan of God. When God said, "Let them make me a sanctuary, that I may dwell among them," He literally said "in" them. God's ultimate goal has always been to dwell within His people (Jer. 31:31–33) and to put His Spirit within us. When you accept Jesus, you become the Mishkan (God's human temple or dwelling place).

11 In Him also, we have obtained an inheritance, being predestined according to the purpose of Him, who works all things according to the counsel of His will,

12 That we who first trusted in Christ should be to the praise of His glory

13 In Him you also trusted, after you heard the Word of truth, the gospel of your salvation; in whom also, having believed, you were sealed with the Holy Spirit of promise,

14 Who is the guarantee of our inheritance until the redemption of the purchased possession, to the praise of His glory? (Eph. 1:11–14)

Jesus answered and said unto him, "If a man loves me, he will keep My word: and my Father will love him, and we will come unto him, and make our abode with him" (John 14:23).

"Behold, I stand at the door and knock: if any man hears my voice and open the door, I will come into him and will sup with him, and he with me" (Rev. 3:20).

The Presence of the Lord is always a pleasant thing and never something to be afraid of for the believer in Christ. When the Spirit came upon Jesus, He came in the form of a dove, which was a symbol of affection and caressing in Israel. When Isaiah saw the throne of God and the King in all His glory (Isaiah 6), he was terrified and expected death at any moment, but when a sacrifice is made, and the blood is present, the loving-kindness and mercy of the Lord are also present, and the people of God are compelled to speak out: "Truly the Lord is good, for His loving-kindness endures forever."

As I reflect on God's blessings in my life, I must say He has bestowed many upon my vessel of clay, though at the time I had no idea what He was doing. Even so, as I obeyed Him with humble, childlike faith, He was continuously bestowing blessing and subtracting or shedding light upon sinful deeds, which were causing harm; those were habits opposed to or not worthy of sharing with a trice-holy God. Many of these supernatural occurrences were so surreal; it wasn't clear what God was bestowing upon me. This is the reason we are told to search the scriptures to learn about God—who He is, and His ways which are past finding out (Rom. 11:33). All these answers are found in the Bible. It behooves us to be industrious and diligently search the scriptures. Satan, on the other hand, makes certain we are preoccupied with the activities of this world (movies, games, current events, wasting time). God tells us, "Take my yoke upon you, and learn of me; for I am meek and lowly in heart: and ye shall find rest unto your souls" (Matt. 11:29). The more knowledge we have about God, the greater will be our peace and comfort because we'll have more power to resist sin and know how to avoid the numerous pitfalls of the enemy. We are assured that no matter what happens during life's journey, Almighty God has our backs, and we can rest in Him (1 Cor. 9:2; Isa. 41:10; Deut. 31:6).

GOD'S TEMPLE

> What? Know ye not that your body is the temple of the Holy Ghost, which is in you, which ye have of God, and ye are not your own? (1 Cor. 6:19)

> If any man defiles the temple of God, he shall God destroy; for the temple of God is holy, which temple ye are. (1 Cor. 3:17)

HOWEVER, HOW MANY of us have smoked cigarettes, drunk alcohol, used recreational drugs, or have overeaten and splurged on desserts or indulged in pork and other foods that God has commanded us to avoid (Leviticus and Deuteronomy 14)? These are but a small example of defiling our inward temple. Satan would have us believe that we are no longer under the law, that it's no harm in eating foods that God called unclean. We must obey God rather than Satan or man. These foods will still defile the temple of God, which dwells within us. God's temple should be treated as sacred. "If any man defiles the temple of God, him shall God destroy; for the temple of God is holy, which temple ye are" (1 Cor. 3:17).

What agreement is there between the temple of God and idols, for we are the temple of the living God. As God has said, "I will live with them and walk among them, and I will be their God, and they will be my peo-ple" (2 Cor. 6:16). It doesn't matter what I did; he only sees me for who I am. He didn't throw David under the bus. David committed murder and adultery. Even so, David knew God and had the heart to agree with God. He ran to God, not away from Him. God knows we are clay vessels, living at the top of hell itself, never free from demonic and wicked influences. God asks us to be real, come to Him with remorseful hearts.

This is one of the reasons King David was so special. God saw the best in David's character and said," He's a man after my own heart (Acts 13:22, 13:21; Deut. 29:19). God loved David's attitude and personality so much, that He established his kingdom forever. "But King Solomon will be blessed, and David's throne will remain secure before the LORD forever." Jesus Himself will rule upon that earthly throne for a thousand years, demonstrating to the whole earth how it should be run (1 Kings 2:45). God was pleased with David's character—his heart. God gives an illustration of the type of character that pleases Him. "Did you tremble at my Word—has not my hand made all these things, and so they came into being?" God declared in His Word, "This is the one I esteem: he who is humble and contrite in spirit and trembles at my word" (Isa. 66:2).

As a king, David was strong and powerful, but his heart always respected and was willing to give first place to Almighty God. On one occasion, men sacrificed their lives to get him a drink of water. David recognized their awesome gift and deemed it too great a sacrifice for him; therefore, he poured the water on the ground, as a gift to the LORD—he said he wasn't worthy of that kind of blessing. Only the Most High has the right to receive such an honor (2 Sam. 23:16). That was David. He was a man of honor. Yes, he did sin many times, as have we all, but David knew to whom he should run when He was wrong. He knew who it was that deserved the highest praises. He wasn't ashamed to dance before the Lord with all his might. He was the king of his nation, but he always remem-bered that God is the King of everything.

As God's Word instructs us, "Grow in grace, and in the knowledge of our Lord and Savior Jesus Christ" (2 Pet. 3:18).

It has taken many years for me to grasp the realization of what was taking place within my human temple. I ponder a time when a young man stood poised before me with a raised machete, ready to come down upon me at any moment; even so, something stopped his savage strike.

He continued standing before me as though transfixed, gazing at something only his demon-possessed glance recognized. And yet, without my having to do anything, this young man, who was so intent on causing me vicious bodily harm, promptly lowered his weapon; his eyes widened, as though staring at something shockingly formidable. He closed his eyes and lowered his head, like a little child being reprimanded by parents for having fallen short of established instructions. Immediately, I discerned something far-reaching had transpired.

I left the scene that day, but the incident has stayed with me, and I've always questioned, "What did that young man see as he stared at my chest? What had this young man witnessed that stopped his brutal act?" It took many years, but now I'm totally aware of what he saw. The demon-possessed young man had witnessed a heavenly scene that caused him to stare so intently at my chest; he saw the Almighty seated upon His earthly throne position within my heart. This was what stopped him dead in his tracks and made him submit to Someone greater.

The Word reminds us to "study to show yourself approved to God, a workman who needs not to be ashamed, rightly dividing the word of truth" (2 Tim. 2:15). We must study and find out just who we are in Christ, and most importantly, we must understand how Satan fears the Christ residing within us. Nevertheless, Christians will remain babies and lose in daily warfare, unless they arm themselves with the whole armor God has given them (Eph. 6:11–18). Satan fears the "Sword of the Spirit" (the Word of God) because it's futile to fight against it. God's Word is settled forever and goes forth to complete all His will. Indeed, Satan doesn't fear man, but he does fear the man who has full knowledge of God's Word, for when he is put in his rightful place: under the feet of humanity. We don't have to argue with Satan, but only be aware of what God's Word says we, His children, are. God's Word lets us know just what Satan is or isn't allowed to do in these daily onslaughts.

For this reason, Satan keeps us preoccupied with worldly concerns (the latest movies and all genres of entertainment, or with drugs, worrying about bills, and other time-consuming pursuits), anything that keeps us out of God's Word. He doesn't want us to know who we are in Christ. The less we know, the more power and control he has over us.

THE ARK OF THE COVENANT

WHAT DID THEY see when the temple was opened? When the secret place was laid bare, what did they see? "There was seen in his temple the ark of his covenant" (Rev. 11:19).

If we could investigate heaven at this moment, this is what we would see: "The ark of his covenant." We would behold our Lord and Savior, Jesus Christ. He is the incarnate God, our great covenant deposit sitting at the right hand of the Father, where the Godhead shines radiantly. Jesus is the Ark of the Covenant to which all the references and shadows in scriptures pointed. He is the Lamb amid the throne, keeping the covenant always close to the heart of the Father.

By faith, we know that God has entered a covenant with us. "He that believeth on the Son hath everlasting life, He that believeth on Him is not condemned." Those believing in Him are at peace with God and have passed from death unto life, and shall never come into condemnation. Believers are in this covenant with God. Those who are repentant sinners, wipe your weeping eyes and ask God to take the dust out of them that you may see that unchanging covenant made with you today and forever. Our beloved Creator fills heaven and earth; the infinite God Almighty condescended to make our hearts His special dwelling place. He is addressed as,

"Thou that dwells between the cherubim." Here is the unrivaled component of the new covenant: "I will dwell in them and walk in them."

It is marvelous that God does speak with men and has taken us into a relationship with Himself in the person of the Lord Jesus Christ, who is at once the second person of the Godhead, and the brother of the sons of men. All believers should rejoice in the covenant that God is no longer separated from men! The split made by sin is filled, the gulf is bridged, and God now dwells with His children, manifesting Himself to us, and "the secret of the Lord is with us that fear him." He is closer to us than our next breath. He is our God, and we are His people forever.

Again, how many chambers are in our heart? Four chambers. Observe the similarities again: there were four cherubs and four Levite priests. It's all there, an earthly representation of what John saw in heaven. "I saw the four beasts and the Ark of the Covenant" (the throne of God); and he said, "I saw twenty-four elders surrounding the throne." Now understand, God made humanity in that fashion. We have twenty-four ribs surrounding the throne of God in our bodies. These ribs represent the twenty-four elders who are seated around God's heavenly throne. God dwells within us. We are really the earthly dwelling place of the living God.

Those unwittingly desecrating God's places of residence were ignominiously killed instantly. Even today, God gives a warning to those who'd desecrate that which He has set apart for Himself. "Touch not my anointed and do my ministers no harm" (1 Chron. 16:22; Ps. 105:15).

Therefore, that young man raising his machete and about to desecrate the dwelling place of Almighty God, the Holy Spirit, was in deep trouble. He saw the very presence of God Almighty dwelling within my inner sanctum (my heart); he could do nothing but put down his weapon, divert his gaze, and pray that God wouldn't send him to hell.

www.ingramcontent.com/pod-product-compliance
Lightning Source LLC
Chambersburg PA
CBHW031242120626
46545CB00003B/1240